JACKSONVILLE
JAGUARS

BY TOM GLAVE

The Child's World®

Published by The Child's World®
1980 Lookout Drive • Mankato, MN 56003-1705
800-599-READ • www.childsworld.com

Acknowledgments
The Child's World®: Mary Berendes, Publishing Director
Red Line Editorial: Editorial direction
The Design Lab: Design
Amnet: Production

Design Element: Dean Bertoncelj/Shutterstock Images
Photographs ©: Marc Serota/AP Images, cover; Al
Messerschmidt Archive/AP Images, 5; Kellen Micah/Icon
Sportswire, 7; David Stluka/AP Images, 9; John Russell/
AP Images, 11; Rob Wilson/Shutterstock Images, 13; Ste-
phen Morton/AP Images, 14-15; Michael S. Green/
AP Images, 17; Phil Coale/AP Images, 19; Phelan
M. Ebenhack/AP Images, 21, 27; ZumaPress/Icon
Sportswire, 23; Stephen Bartholomew/Actionplus/Icon
Sportswire, 25; Cliff Welch/Icon Sportswire, 29

ISBN 9781631439971   662 1875
LCCN 2014959702

Printed in the United States of America
Mankato, MN
July, 2015
PA02265

ABOUT THE AUTHOR

Tom Glave grew up watching football on TV and playing it in the field next to his house. He learned to write about sports at the University of Missouri–Columbia and has written for newspapers in New Jersey, Missouri, Arkansas, and Texas. He lives near Houston, Texas, and cannot wait to play backyard football with his kids Tommy, Lucas, and Allison.

TABLE OF CONTENTS

GO, JAGUARS!   4

WHO ARE THE JAGUARS?   6

WHERE THEY CAME FROM   8

WHO THEY PLAY   10

WHERE THEY PLAY   12

THE FOOTBALL FIELD   14

BIG DAYS   16

TOUGH DAYS   18

MEET THE FANS   20

HEROES THEN   22

HEROES NOW   24

GEARING UP   26

SPORTS STATS   28

GLOSSARY   30

FIND OUT MORE   31

INDEX   32

GO, JAGUARS!

The Jacksonville Jaguars had quick success. They made the **playoffs** in just their second season. Jacksonville made the playoffs often for a while. But the Jaguars have had some tough years, too. Fans still love them, though. The fans enjoy that Jacksonville's home stadium has a pool. They can swim while watching "the Jags." Let's meet the Jaguars.

Wide receivers Jimmy Smith (82) and Keenan McCardell (87) both made the Pro Bowl with Jacksonville.

WHO ARE THE JAGUARS?

The Jacksonville Jaguars play in the National Football **League** (NFL). They are one of the 32 teams in the NFL. The NFL includes the American Football Conference (AFC) and the National Football Conference (NFC). The winner of the AFC plays the winner of the NFC in the **Super Bowl**. The Jaguars play in the South Division of the AFC. They have never made the Super Bowl. Only three other current teams have not played in the big game.

Jaguars linebacker Paul Posluszny returns an interception during a game against the Buffalo Bills on December 2, 2012.

WHERE THEY CAME FROM

Businessman Tom Petway loved the NFL. He wanted a team in north Florida. Petway started a group in 1989 to make it happen. The group applied for an **expansion** team for Jacksonville. The team name was chosen before the Jaguars even existed. Jacksonville was awarded a team in 1993. The Jaguars started playing in 1995. Their first preseason game was against the Carolina Panthers. The Panthers also joined the NFL in 1995.

Quarterback Mark Brunell runs with the ball during Jacksonville's first preseason game, which was played against fellow 1995 NFL expansion team the Carolina Panthers.

WHO THEY PLAY

The Jacksonville Jaguars play 16 games each season. With so few games, each one is important. Every year, the Jaguars play two games against each of the other three teams in their division. Those teams are the Tennessee Titans, Houston Texans, and Indianapolis Colts. The Jaguars also play six other teams from the AFC and four from the NFC. Jacksonville and Tennessee are rivals. The Titans beat the Jaguars twice during the 1999 regular season. Then Tennessee beat Jacksonville again in the playoffs. Those were Jacksonville's only losses that year.

The Jaguars and Titans have had some tough AFC South battles over the years.

WHERE THEY PLAY

Jacksonville plays at EverBank Field. It used to be called Jacksonville Municipal Stadium. The Jaguars first played there on August 18, 1995. No other NFL team had played its first game in a brand-new stadium. EverBank normally holds 67,246 fans. Extra seats can be added for big events. That makes room for more than 82,000 people. The stadium also hosts college football games. The Super Bowl was played there after the 2004 season.

Jacksonville lost its first NFL game 10-3 to the Houston Oilers at home on September 3, 1995.

THE FOOTBALL FIELD

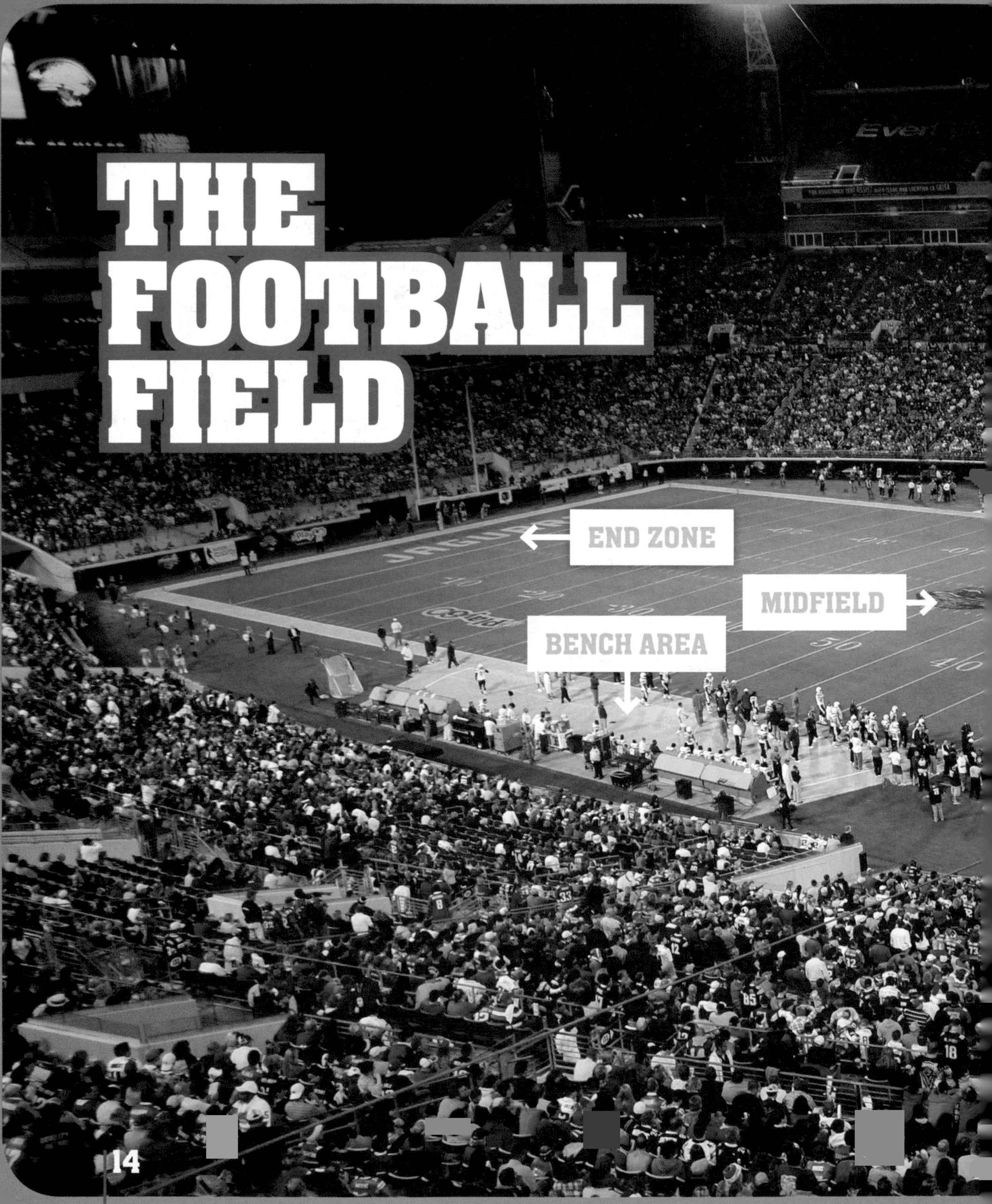

END ZONE

MIDFIELD

BENCH AREA

HASH MARKS

SIDELINE

GOAL POST

GOAL LINE

20-YARD LINE

END LINE

BIG DAYS

The Jaguars have had some great moments in their history. Here are three of the greatest:

1996—It was the Jaguars' second season. They won their last five regular-season games. That took them to the playoffs. Jacksonville upset the Buffalo Bills and Denver Broncos. Jacksonville then lost the AFC Championship Game. But fans were happy with the team's early success.

1999—The Jaguars won 11 straight games. They finished 14-2 and won the AFC Central. Jacksonville played the Miami Dolphins in the playoffs on January 15, 2000. The Jaguars won 62-7. Only one team had scored more points in a playoff game through 2014.

Jaguars quarterback Mark Brunell celebrates after Jacksonville's 30-27 playoff upset of the Denver Broncos on January 4, 1997.

2007—Jacksonville beat the Pittsburgh Steelers in two big games. Running back Fred Taylor scored late in a regular-season win. It helped the Jaguars make the playoffs. There the teams met on January 5, 2008. Jacksonville trailed 29-28. There was less than two minutes to go. Quarterback David Garrard ran for 32 yards on fourth down. That set up the winning field goal.

TOUGH DAYS

Football is a hard game. Even the best teams have rough games and seasons. Here are some of the toughest times in Jaguars history:

2000—Jacksonville had made four straight playoff appearances. So fans had big expectations.
But **injuries** slowed the Jaguars. Quarterback Mark Brunell was **sacked** 54 times. The Jaguars finished 7-9.

2002—Jacksonville ended the year 6-10. Coach Tom Coughlin had been the Jaguars' only coach. But he was fired after the season. Through 2014, Jacksonville has just two playoff appearances since.

2008—The Jaguars suffered more injuries. Several offensive linemen were hurt early on. Then star running

Tom Coughlin was fired after Jacksonville's 6–10 season in 2002.

back Fred Taylor injured his thumb. Jacksonville had
been in the top ten in scoring the previous two seasons.
But they placed 24th in 2008. The team finished 5–11.
Taylor left the team after the season.

MEET THE FANS

Jaguars fans have fun at games. They can swim in the stadium's pool while watching. Fans like to chant "Duval" during games. That is the county in which the team plays. Jaxson de Ville is Jacksonville's mascot. He is a yellow cat with teal spots. He plays football with children during halftime. Jacksonville also has fans in London, England. The Jaguars have played several games there.

Mascot Jaxson de Ville leads the Jaguars onto the field before a preseason game on August 10, 2012.

HEROES THEN

Offensive lineman Tony Boselli was Jacksonville's first draft pick. He went to five **Pro Bowls** in seven years with the team. Quarterback Mark Brunell topped the NFL in passing yards in 1996. Brunell led the team to four straight playoff appearances. Running back Fred Taylor was quick. He rushed for more than 1,000 yards seven times as a Jaguar. Running back Maurice Jones-Drew was also great. He had 8,071 rushing yards over eight years. Wide receiver Jimmy Smith led the NFL in receptions in 1999.

Running back Maurice Jones-Drew led the NFL with 1,606 rushing yards in 2011.

HEROES NOW

Quarterback Blake Bortles was drafted in 2014. Four weeks into that season he was named the starter. Denard Robinson was a quarterback in college. But he is a running back in the NFL. He is small and shifty. That makes him tough to tackle. Safety Jonathan Cyprien was Jacksonville's second-highest tackler as a **rookie** in 2013. Linebacker Paul Posluszny led the team in tackles that year. He also made the Pro Bowl in 2013.

Running back Denard Robinson (left) takes a handoff from quarterback Blake Bortles during a game against the Dallas Cowboys in London, England, on November 9, 2014.

GEARING UP

NFL players wear team uniforms. They wear helmets and pads to keep them safe. Cleats help them make quick moves and run fast. Some players wear extra gear for protection.

THE FOOTBALL

NFL footballs are made of leather. Under the leather is a lining that fills with air to give the ball its shape. The leather has bumps or "pebbles." These help players grip the ball. Laces help players control their throws. Footballs are also called "pigskins" because some of the first balls were made from pig bladders. Today they are made of leather from cows.

Wide receiver Allen Robinson tries to get open during a game against the Cleveland Browns on October 19, 2014.

HELMET

SHOULDER PADS

GLOVES

THIGH PADS

FOOTBALL

CLEATS

SPORTS STATS

ere are some of the all-time career records for the Jacksonville Jaguars. All the stats are through the 2014 season.

PASSING YARDS

Mark Brunell 25,698

David Garrard 16,003

INTERCEPTIONS

Rashean Mathis 30

Aaron Beasley 15

RECEPTIONS

Jimmy Smith 862

Keenan McCardell 499

SACKS

Tony Brackens 55

Joel Smeenge 34

TOTAL TOUCHDOWNS

Maurice Jones-Drew 81

Fred Taylor 70

POINTS

Josh Scobee 1,022

Mike Hollis 764

Running back Fred Taylor made the Pro Bowl after the 2007 season.

RUSHING YARDS

Fred Taylor 11,271

Maurice Jones-Drew 8,071

GLOSSARY

expansion when a league grows by adding a team or teams

injuries when players get hurt

league an organization of sports teams that compete against each other

playoffs a series of games after the regular season that decides which two teams play in the Super Bowl

Pro Bowls the NFL's All-Star game, in which the best players in the league compete

rookie a player playing in his first season

sacked when the quarterback is tackled behind the line of scrimmage before he can throw the ball

Super Bowl the championship game of the NFL, played between the winners of the AFC and the NFC

FIND OUT MORE

IN THE LIBRARY

Frisch, Nate. *The Story of the Jacksonville Jaguars.*
Mankato, MN: Creative Education, 2014.

Gilbert, Sara. *The Story of the NFL.*
Mankato, MN: Creative Education, 2011.

Stewart, Mark. *The Jacksonville Jaguars.*
Chicago: Norwood House, 2013.

ON THE WEB

Visit our Web site for links about the Jacksonville Jaguars:
childsworld.com/links

Note to Parents, Teachers, and Librarians: We routinely verify our Web links to make sure they are safe and active sites. So encourage your readers to check them out!

INDEX

AFC Central, 16
AFC South, 6, 10, 16
American Football
  Conference (AFC), 6, 18

Bortles, Blake, 24
Boselli, Tony, 22
Brunell, Mark, 18, 22
Buffalo Bills, 16

Carolina Panthers, 8
Coughlin, Tom, 18
Cyprien, Jonathan, 24

Denver Broncos, 16
"Duval," 20

EverBank Field, 4, 12, 20

Garrard, David, 17

Houston Texans, 10

Indianapolis Colts, 10

Jaxson de Ville (mascot), 20
Jones-Drew, Maurice, 22

London, England, 20

Miami Dolphins, 16

National Football Conference
  (NFC), 6
National Football League
  (NFL), 6, 8, 12, 22, 24, 26

Petway, Tom, 8
Pittsburgh Steelers, 17
Posluszny, Paul, 24

Robinson, Denard, 24

Smith, Jimmy, 22
Super Bowl, 6, 12

Taylor, Fred, 17, 19, 22
Tennessee Titans, 10